Learning to Read, Step by Step!

Ready to Read   Preschool–Kindergarten
• big type and easy words • rhyme and rhythm • picture clues
For children who know the alphabet and are eager to begin reading.

Reading with Help   Preschool–Grade 1
• basic vocabulary • short sentences • simple stories
For children who recognize familiar words and sound out new words with help.

Reading on Your Own   Grades 1–3
• engaging characters • easy-to-follow plots • popular topics
For children who are ready to read on their own.

Reading Paragraphs   Grades 2–3
• challenging vocabulary • short paragraphs • exciting stories
For newly independent readers who read simple sentences with confidence.

Ready for Chapters   Grades 2–4
• chapters • longer paragraphs • full-color art
For children who want to take the plunge into chapter books but still like colorful pictures.

STEP INTO READING® is designed to give every child a successful reading experience. The grade levels are only guides; children will progress through the steps at their own speed, developing confidence in their reading.

Remember, a lifetime love of reading starts with a single step!

To water-loving Wyatt
–M.K.

The editors would like to thank Paul L. Sieswerda, Aquarium Curator (retired), New York Aquarium, for his assistance in the preparation of this book.

Visit us on the Web!
StepIntoReading.com
randomhouse.com/kids

Educators and librarians, for a variety of teaching tools, visit us at
RHTeachersLibrarians.com

ISBN 978-0-553-49901-8 (trade) — ISBN 978-0-553-49902-5 (lib. bdg.) —
ISBN 978-0-553-49903-2 (ebook)

Printed in the United States of America
10 9 8 7 6 5 4 3

Wild Sea Creatures
Sharks, Whales, and Dolphins!

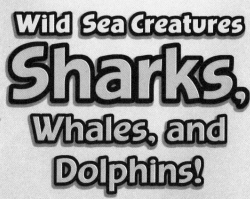

by Martin Kratt and Chris Kratt

Random House 🏠 New York

What if you could do
what sea creatures do?
You could eat, swim,
and live underwater.

We are the Wild Kratts.
Get ready to activate
Creature Powers
and dive deep with us.

Tiger Sharks!

Tiger sharks have stripes on their sides.

Tiger sharks are predators.
A predator eats other
animals.
Tiger sharks like to eat
sea turtles.

Sea Turtles!

Sea turtles are reptiles.
They have tough shells
to protect them from harm.

"It is like a shield,"
Martin tells Chris.

Sperm Whales!

Sperm whales are
one of the biggest kinds
of whales.
A baby sperm whale
is very big, too.

Martin says, "Let's take
a deep breath
and get ready to dive!"

Sperm whales breathe air
but can dive very deep.
They can swim to
the bottom of the sea
in search of their
favorite food, squid.

Colossal Squid!

Whales and squids
have big battles.
Squids fight with arms
and long tentacles.
But the whales usually
win and eat the squids!

"Squid hug!" says Martin.

Blowfish!

Blowfish look like
ordinary fish.
Then they blow up!

They become round, spiny, and too big for predators to swallow.

Yeti Crabs!

Yeti crabs live
deep in the dark sea.
These small crabs have "hairs"
on their legs and claws.
The hairs help them catch
little bits of food to eat.

"What's on the menu?"
Martin asks.

Dolphins!

Dolphins are always
on the go.

Dolphins swim.

Dolphins jump.

Dolphins round up fish to eat.

And watch out for sharks!

Great White Sharks!

Great white sharks are the biggest hunting sharks. They have large, sharp teeth and a keen sense of smell. They hunt alone, and they like to eat dolphins!

Dolphins work together
to fight back.

Great white sharks
never stop swimming.
They live in oceans
around the world.

"Let's keep moving!"
Chris cheers.

Moray Eels!

Moray eels live in
rock and coral caves.
They are predators.
They eat fish.

This moray eel does not see
the frogfish that is hiding.
Do you?
Frogfish blend in
with their habitat.

Flying Fish!

Some fish swim fast.

Other fish hide.

And some fish fly to escape
from predators.

Flying fish use their fins
to glide into the air!

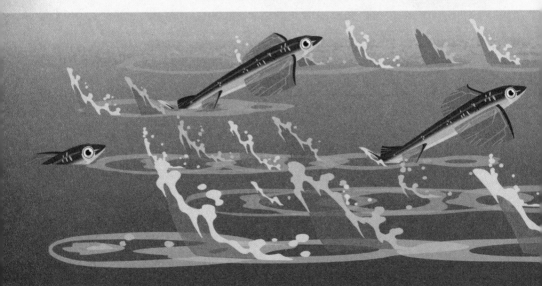

But that
doesn't mean
these fish
are safe!

"You got me, bro!"
says Martin.
Go, Creature Powers!